I LOVE JESUS, BUT...

EMBRACING THE TENSION BETWEEN FAITH AND MENTAL HEALTH

A COLLECTION OF ESSAYS BY

ROBERT VORE & STEVE AUSTIN

ISBN-13: 978-1544258225

I LOVE

EMBRACING THE TENSION

JESUS,

BETWEEN FAITH & MENTAL HEALTH

BUT...

A COLLECTION OF ESSAYS BY

ROBERT VORE
& STEVE AUSTIN

HOSTS OF CXMH

I LOVE JESUS, BUT...

ABOUT ROBERT VORE

 Robert has worked for various ministries & nonprofits in Georgia, Alabama, Florida, and England. His writing has been featured on websites such as The Mighty, Thought Catalog, and Patheos. Robert speaks at youth groups, schools, and more. He is also a QPR Suicide Prevention Instructor for groups of any size. Robert is currently working towards his Masters in Clinical Mental Health Counseling. He lives in Atlanta with his wife and dog.

ABOUT STEVE AUSTIN

Steve is the author of several books, including the Amazon bestseller, *From Pastor to a Psych Ward*, plus *Self Care for the Wounded Soul: 21 Days of Messy Grace*. Abuse, addiction, and a suicide attempt weren't the end of Steve's story. In fact, a suicide attempt is where his life began. Steve blogs regularly at graceismessy.com, and is also a self-care coach (jointheselfcarechallenge.com), sign language interpreter, and worship pastor. But his favorite role is family man. Lindsey, Ben Thomas, and Caroline make his life so much sweeter.

Robert Vore and Steve Austin are the hosts of CXMH: A Podcast at the Intersection of Christianity and Mental Health. They love to speak together on suicide prevention, self-care, and anything else that involves life at the intersection of faith and mental health. Email cxmhpodcast@gmail.com today to schedule a workshop, lecture, or retreat.

I LOVE JESUS, BUT...

FOREWORD

"I love Jesus, but...."

It's something we all say isn't it? I've lost count of the number of times I've said it. And the reason we say it is very simple - life isn't perfect, and we're not perfect. We suffer. We struggle.

Robert and Steve share vulnerably and with great candidness in this book their own struggles, are very frank about their own imperfections, and how they've wrestled with these type of questions.

The reason their answers hold such authority, is that they speak from experience. They've been there. They've had struggles with addiction, mental health, and all their consequences. As someone who has struggled with similar issues, I found myself feeling safe, and that someone, somewhere, finally understood the struggles I've had.

This book helped me to realise I'm not alone. And it gave me renewed hope of a new tomorrow. It reminded me again that resurrection is possible, even in the darkest of dark days.

And what I love most about the book, is the it's ideas are built on the foundation of grace. Robert and Steve begin this book with grace. With the truth that all of us are enough, just as we are. The truth that God knows and sees us with all our imperfections, and in *that* space, tells us we are enough, and we are beloved.

This book will give you hope. Hope that if we can receive the truth of our own value, even in our place of deep brokenness, we can begin to see ourselves as God sees us. It will give you the hope that if we begin to care for ourselves, love ourselves, and see ourselves through God's eyes, we can have our lives transformed.

And then, in the words of the old hymn, grace truly will have led us home.

James Prescott
Author, 'Mosaic Of Grace - God's Beautiful Reshaping Of Our Broken Lives'

I LOVE JESUS, BUT...

WELCOME HOME

I know.

I mean, I can't fully know your story, but I do know this: you've lived through things that sucked. At times you were drowning and saw no way out.

Mine feels like a lifetime ago, and yet, as close as a blink. The flashing lights, the incoherent sounds, the nurses' scrubs are all a blur. I remember being blank and cold and utterly confused. The hospital blanket, fresh out of the warmer, was my only comfort.

For years, I thought grace was just part of an old melody I would hum as I did my homework. But grace is stronger than any other force in life. Grace is why you're still here. *And grace will lead you home.*

Your situation may be different, but, like us, you've come out on the other side somehow. *Welcome.* You're alive and you're breathing.

Tell your story loud and clear, because there are those around you silently walking through the parts of their story that suck, and they need to know they aren't the only ones. They need to know there's light on the other side. They need to know that you're alive and you're breathing.

Or maybe you're not there yet. You're still in the

suck. Maybe you're not convinced there's a light on the other side and you're pretty sure there's no coming back this time.

But there is. There is hope and there is life, even after your very worst moments.

The maze of finding faith in the midst of mental health is winding, frustrating, and so exhausting. It usually includes counseling, church, intense therapy, prayers, new meds, and lots and lots of embarrassing honesty. But you will make it. You'll find the strength to admit you are weak. It will make you a new person.

I know there are days that feel too heavy to get out of bed. I know there are moments that feel as if your heart has been ripped from your chest and I know that it seems like it would be easier to give up.

Find the people around you that you trust to love you well. Let them speak your pain loudly and clearly. Because there are people who want to help you carry it. There are people who want nothing more than to walk alongside you, to bear its weight with and for you, to hold you up when you collapse, and tell you to keep going.

So, to you:

Don't give up. *Keep going.*
Don't give up. *There is light.*
Don't give up. *There is hope.*

11

And there is grace. Right here, in the pages of this tiny little book. Grace has found you and it will not let you go. You are not a lost cause, and your life isn't over. Actually, your life is just about to begin. All of those years you were running and hiding and working so hard to keep your game face on – all of that was death. What happens next is *life*. You don't have to do anything to find grace or deserve it. You just need to accept it, to show up for it.

Share your story.
Listen.
Love well.
Never give up.

The only way to push back against stigma and bad theology is to embrace the tension between faith and mental health. Jesus lives in the tension. And so do we.

Welcome home,

Robert and Steve

I LOVE JESUS, BUT...

CONTENTS

I LOVE JESUS, BUT...

1

...BUT I STILL NEED MEDICATIONS

Steve:

After two days of panic attacks and a scary spike in my blood pressure, I left work early and drove myself to the doctor's office, full of shame and anxiety. Every stop light seemed to make it worse. Although I don't normally have road rage, the little old lady in front of me was making my forehead sweat.

Once I arrived, the doctor adjusted my meds and took me off caffeine. I have loved coffee for 15 years, but I have followed the rules for six weeks. And I feel much better for it.

Living with mental illness means knowing your triggers, respecting your limits, and following the doctor's orders, even if they are less than convenient. Once a week, living with mental illness means throwing all caution to the wind and savoring the rich smell and the taste of every single drop of my one cup of real coffee.

Hold the cream and sugar. None of that mocha-chocha-bullshit, please.

Sometimes living with mental illness means not fully comprehending the simple joy of your own beautiful children. It's going to bed and praying you fall asleep

16

before your thoughts begin to swirl and you fall apart. It's seeing sleep as a chance to escape instead of rest.

Mental illness sounds scary to some people. It's misunderstood by most. But for me, it's life. It's a daily struggle, but one worth fighting. There are days I feel like a science experiment, trying each med my doctor prescribes, hoping one of them will make life normal again. Sometimes the med works for a while and stops. So I travel back to the doctor's office for another visit and sort through my laundry list of side effects.

With both mental illness and cancer, you can't see the disease. But, while it is perfectly ok for a cancer patient to have chemo, it is not always acceptable for someone with a mental illness to take a prescription to address the chemical imbalance that dramatically affects their life. I long for the day when I can comfortably say, *my hope is built on nothing less than Jesus' blood and good prescription drugs.*

I had plenty of hard days before my suicide attempt. But afterward, I wondered if I would ever be a value-added member of any community again. I constantly struggled with my diagnosis, believing I would never feel normal again. I remember looking into my little boy's innocent and curious blue eyes, pleading with God to save him from his own father. Wrestling with relationships was one of the hardest battles of all, but not nearly as difficult as wrestling with my faith. How can one feel faithful in light of

17

depression and anxiety? The thing to remember is that the hard days after the attempt are no different than the hard days before the attempt. They are hard days. And sometimes they really suck.

The truth is, hard days are not different before or after the crisis has ended, but the person who attempted suicide is certainly different. They have tasted death. They've traveled to the bottom of the barrel and know what rock bottom feels like. For me, it was the latching of the large metal door, which locked me in the bowels of the hospital. Someone recovering from a suicide attempt knows what the end of the rope looks like. But they are still alive, still holding on, caught between secretly hoping the strands fray so disappear beneath the sinking sand, or wishing their feet could just touch solid ground.

For me, the hard days still come, but I know what to do with them now. I'm able to recognize shame for the liar it is. I know to let the emotions wash in and recede, like a tide. I know there is an ebb and flow to life, even life that includes triggers and trauma. I have learned to no longer read my emotions as the only truth.

At the end of a hard day, I am stronger for having faced my struggles head-on. I put the car in drive and I head home–to my safe place, my comfort zone, my support system–and I rest. Hard days will come again, but as I drive, I know those good days will come too.

Robert:

I take medication for my mental health, too. I've been on ADHD medication for a few years and although I don't take them currently, I have taken antidepressants as well. I mention this because I've talked to what seems like an increasingly large amount of people recently who believe that taking medication for your brain is somehow anti-Jesus or anti-Christian.

Of course I believe Jesus has the power to heal a mental illness. I also believe He has the power to cure a headache. Or diabetes. Or cancer. So why is it we don't see people billing those as purely spiritual problems and refusing to take medication?

Mental health is unfamiliar and uncomfortable and, often, downright scary. But I would argue that, in large part, it's because we refuse to talk about it, which contributes to the stigma and shame surrounding it. We can't learn about things we don't discuss.

The medicinal routes for mental illnesses aren't 100% foolproof. Neither are cancer treatments or headache medication or anything else. (Have you seen the side effects list on most medications?)

Speaking of headaches: I get them a lot. I go through months where I get at least one headache a day. This obviously isn't ideal, and I end up taking a fair amount of medication during these times. Like, the several-headache-pills-per-day amount.

And can we talk about allergy medications? For the past month or so, when I don't take allergy medication in the morning, I spend the rest of the day sneezing, my throat hurting, and my head feeling foggy. In fact, last week I was at a party with some friends and we were outside most of the time. The allergy medication I had taken that morning was starting to wear off, so I felt miserable for the last hour or so I was there.

What these things both have in common is that *I can't function very well* when my head is pounding or I'm constantly sneezing. I couldn't enjoy myself at the party, I can't hold very long conversations; honestly, I can't do much of anything.

When my head is hurting or my allergies are killing me, I'm not fully me. I'm not at my best. I can't talk to people or build relationships or love them well. When I'm in pain, I can't do the things I believe God has created me to do. As a result, I believe that God would approve of me using the miracle of modern medicine to help resolve those issues.

But I've never heard anyone claim that headaches or allergies are a spiritual problem. I've never heard someone refuse to take Advil or Claritin or any other number of things because 'that would mean trusting God less. I've known people that hated taking all medicines for various reasons, but I've never heard it justified with the name of Jesus.

As hard as it is to do the things I believe God has created me to do with a headache and allergies, they've got nothing on how my mental health can slow me down. When I don't take my ADHD medication, I can't focus on a conversation. How can I show love to a person when I can't absorb what they're saying? When I'm in the deepest depths of depression, I am apathetic about everything. It's not that I *don't* care, it's that I *can't*. Does that sound like someone who's loving others the way Jesus asks us to?

When I don't take medication for my mental health, I cannot be who I believe God wants me to be. So I don't think medication is a slap in the face of God, I think it's trusting Him more. If you and I can believe that God works through surgeons and physicians and nurses to help heal us, can't we believe the same about psychiatrists and counselors? My God is big enough to reach even psychopharmacology. My God can use miracles and love and community and *yes, medication* to help.

So for all the reasons I could avoid taking medication, I have better reasons to embrace it.

I'll keep taking headache medicine until I can figure out what's causing them and then I'll work to learn how to avoid them. The same applies for mental health medication.

I once heard it described like this: if counseling is a

journey from Point A to Point B (where the journey is learning how to better handle your emotions and avoid situations that are unhealthy for you), then when your brain chemistry isn't working the way is should be, you're starting in a hole. It's impossible to walk anywhere while you're stuck in a hole, so you need a ladder to get on the level ground. Only once you're there can you start the journey.

I believe in a God that wants us to be healthy and whole, a God who wants us to live our lives fully and free. He works through miracles, He works through medical professionals, and He works through medication.

Reflection:

When the shame of being prescribed medications for your mental health whispers lies in your ear, what is one positive way you can speak back with life-giving truth about who you are?

I LOVE JESUS, BUT...

2

...BUT MY RELATIONSHIPS ARE SUFFERING

By: Steve Austin

Relationships are tough. Adding mental illness to the mix can really muddy the waters. People who don't have a mental illness sometimes have a very hard time seeing things the way we do.

After living through my wife's hospitalization with postpartum depression, plus my own stay in ICU and a psych ward after a serious suicide attempt, I've learned a thing or two about navigating the maze of relationships and mental health. Here's some advice from a guy who's been there:

1) Stop trying to fix your friend or loved one.

I am not my wife's therapist and she isn't mine. While we play a primary role in each other's support systems, we are not professional helpers.

On the days when Lindsey comes home and finds the fog of depression lying low on the living room couch, she has learned to just say, "I'm sorry you're having a tough day. I'm here if you need me." It is not healthy for either of us personally, or for our relationship, for her to do any more than that. It isn't her job to try and fix me or convince me that she's going to be there for me. After all, she proves that by staying.

2) Talk about it with each other.

There is great power in being able to tell our stories, either to our partner, a counselor, or a trusted friend. Being able to name our pain, our struggles and frustrations, and even our greatest hopes is a catalyst toward true change.

But talking about it requires wisdom. Five minutes after someone has a meltdown may not be the best time to work things out. Sometimes you step away with a hurt heart, with the full intention of waking up and talking about it once things settle down.

3) Know your limits.

Each relationship is unique, especially where mental illness is concerned. You have to take a serious look at your situation, self, and sanity. Decide what is best for you and the person you care about. Sometimes the best way to love and honor everyone involved is to take a step back.

4) Love beyond the labels.

The friends and loved ones of someone with a mental illness often suffer in silence. When the person you care about can't explain *why* normal life feels so hard, it is frustrating. We know their labels, we've read all about their symptoms. Labels are important from a medical standpoint, because they show professionals the best course of treatment. But labels in a relationship can be detrimental. Don't become so stuck on them that you forget to love the person in front of you.

5) No more comparisons.

No relationship is perfect. Let go of what you think it is supposed to be, and live in the relationship you actually have. Stop trying to mimic friendships on t.v. No relationship is "normal" and all relationships are hard work.

6) Cry together.

Recently, I picked up my son from daycare with a dog, a Christmas surprise. Everything was great and I was his hero for the day. But as I went to bed that night, I burst into tears. Three years earlier, I missed his first birthday because of my suicide attempt.

At times the guilt still gets the best of me.

Instead of trying to fix anything, Lindsey held my hand and cried with me. Her words were soothing to my soul. She said, "I rarely think about that first birthday. What I do think about are all the memories we have created in the years since. I can't help but think that our relationship would have never become this deep if we hadn't walked through such a living hell together."

7) Look for opportunities to laugh together.

Life tries to get the very best of us, and sometimes, it works. Whether you are the one in ICU or the spouse sitting at the end of the hospital bed, life is full of experiences that leave us questioning our decisions and even our sanity.

Learning to laugh together is powerful medication. Whether it's finding a weekly show you both enjoy or laughing at your kids' silliness, I believe laughter is an extremely powerful tool for remaining connected and finding joy in life.

8) Take care of yourself.

Relationships are stressful, no matter what. But being close to a person with mental illness is a different level. Take time for yourself. Sometimes it's impossible to leave your responsibilities. In that case, find moments of quiet to enjoy something simple – a cup of tea, a few pages of a book – even within your routine. Give yourself space to breathe. It matters.

9) Be Honest

When something frustrates you, speak up. There's nothing worse than an old sore that's been left to fester. If something hurts your feelings, say so. Nobody wants to have to dig to find out why you're pouting.

Just follow this simple rule: tell the truth in love. It's always the right choice.

Reflection:

What's one step you could take today toward embracing the tension of caring about someone who has a mental illness?

If you know someone whose struggles make them a danger to themselves or others, here are some resources:

- Postpartum Depression: 1(800) PPD-MOMS
- National Suicide Prevention Hotline: 1 (800) 273-8255
- National Alliance on Mental Illness

I LOVE JESUS, BUT...

3

...BUT MY PASTOR DOESN'T GET IT

By: Robert Vore

Dear Pastors:

Please be aware.

Be aware of the things you say. When you talk in general terms about depression or anxiety, even when you mean the general emotions, you need to be aware.

Know that there are people in your audience who hear you talk about these things and they hear that their diagnosable, clinical disorder is their fault. They hear you say their anxiety stems from a lack of faith or their depression comes from not finding enough joy. In those words, what they really here is this: "you are a failure. You are not good enough. This is your fault."

The thing is, when you're fighting everyday to get out of bed and interact with people and to just. keep. going. some part of you (you can call it the Enemy if you'd like) gets really good at latching onto those thoughts and repeating them. *Yes, you are a failure. No, you're not good enough. Yes, it's your fault.*

I know that's not what you're trying to say. I'm not asking you to stop hating people with mental health struggles, because I don't believe you do. Instead, I'm asking you to be aware of the way people around you struggling with their mental health will hear your words.

This isn't about being politically correct so you don't offend people. It's knowing the people you serve might get stuck in their head for days and weeks at a time. The very people you have have devoted your life to serving, can easily believe they're not good enough for God, just because they can't muster up some nonstop sense of joy.

And that can be a matter of life and death.

So be aware of the things you say. Also, be aware of your limitations.

In 1 Corinthians, Paul tells us we're *one body, made up of different parts.* That means it's probably going to be someone else's job to help your congregant find mental health. It's your role to help them make sense of their faith and their God as they struggle. Part of being in a healthy community is knowing that we play different roles, that no one person can offer everything.

I know people come to you for help. You hear it all. But the truth is that you aren't trained to counsel people through major mental health crises alone, just like you aren't trained to give someone surgery. Love them, encourage them, and listen to them when they need to share their pain.

And sometimes, your help isn't enough. That's not a criticism of you, it's an opportunity for you to show them Jesus even more. You have a chance to sacrifice your pride, and admit there are things beyond your competency, for the sake of the people you're leading. That's love. It's your responsibility to help steer them towards the professional help they need and deserve.

But don't let that stop you from talking about mental health in the church. Why? Because if Jesus is in the business of stepping into people's pain and shedding light into the darkest places, then the church must be in the same business. This requires both our willingness to put our dark parts out for others to see, and others' willingness to engage with it (and vice versa). People can't carry your burdens if you don't confess them. If we are to be a church that actually brings our weariness and burdens, it takes all of us. Giving and receiving love.

Talking about mental health in the church lets people know they are not alone. In the United States alone, one in four adults experience mental illness in any given year (NAMI). That means there's a good chance someone sitting beside you in church, in your small group or ministry, or volunteering in your leadership is fighting for mental health. That applies to your staff, too (Twenty-three percent of pastors admit to struggling with mental health themselves, according to LifeWay.)

What does it take for people to feel like they're not alone fighting for mental health? We need to share more honestly within the church. The more we listen to the stories and struggles of others, the less isolated we feel. Leading researchers suggest one of the key factors in suicidal feelings and attempts is isolation. Inclusion is not about political correctness. It's a matter of life and death.

In general, we all avoid the things that make us uncomfortable. While that makes for a nice, neat sermon series and uncontroversial small group topics, it also leaves a gap in our congregation's ability to handle suffering. Jesus defines love by His sacrifice, and Paul calls us to carry each other's burdens. If the hallmark of cruciform love is giving of ourselves, we need to sacrifice our discomfort in awkward conversations for the sake of saving lives.

I wholeheartedly believe if the people leading our churches and ministries can be more aware of their language and take on the hard conversations, the Church as a whole can become a much safer place for those wrestling with mental health.

And that's what we want to create, right? Safe spaces, where we can all love and be loved, while we grow and heal and become whole in Christ. Places we can call home.

Reflection:

What's one immediate step you can take toward making your faith family more of a safe place for those affected by mental illness?

I LOVE JESUS, BUT...

4

...BUT GOD HASN'T HEALED ME.

By: Steve Austin

Life comes with losers and leavers and mothers-in-law we'd love to leave in a cloud of dust at the end of a long dirt road. But if we're lucky, we also find the grace to keep living. To take another step. To lean into the mess and not miss out on the full spectrum of the human experience.

Right smack in the middle of the mess is where we most often find grace.

For years, my life was marked by shame and fear. It's true for most victims of childhood sexual assault. I feared turning into my abuser, or realizing I was gay. And in the day-to-day, I feared the person closest to me: my wife. I was terrified Lindsey would discover just how screwed up I actually am, and decide I was not enough. Not man enough. Not strong enough. Not healed enough. Not committed enough. Not holy enough. Not sane enough. Not enough. I was scared that I would be unfaithful to her. I was scared of all of it. As irrational as it is, I would have rather died than face my shame.

Little did I know, my wife would be the tangible grace of God to me.

Anxiety has been my constant companion for as long as I can remember. For several years, I lived under a cloud of shame because of it. I believed I would never find true belonging if anyone knew the real issues I faced on a daily basis.

After my life fell apart and I tried to die, Lindsey stayed with me. Stuck with me like glue. I didn't want anyone to know my story, or the details of the journey that eventually landed me in an ICU. I didn't want my family to know, and I certainly didn't want to face the Church. Like so many others, I thought life came with two choices: be a normal Christian guy, or be crazy. I felt stuck. Lost.

When I had given up on myself, my wife's faith in me became stubborn. Her trust in God is strong as steel. Others didn't understand, couldn't understand, or didn't care. But Lindsey climbed down into the muck with me and refused to let me go. It wasn't easy. Wading through that mess never is. Shame has a way of choking the living right out of life.

After I was released from ICU and the psych ward, Lindsey and I went through months of intense marriage counseling and individual therapy. This is where healing began. The day our marriage counselor connected the dots between my abuse, nearly twenty years of addiction to pornography, and my suicide attempt changed my life forever. She helped us both see that shame was at the core of all of this. It felt like I had just left the optometrist for the first time with a new pair of glasses. Suddenly, I could see individual leaves on trees, instead of blurry shapes and shades of green. All at once my life began to make sense.

My life today is more open and more hopeful than it was. I hid the abuse for so long and my unintentional habit is still to hide. My gut response is to escape. To not show up. But the grace of God calls forth courage, and I practice forming the new habit of opening myself to safe people, creating practical boundaries, and intentionally loosening the grip of shame, a little at a time. For me, for my wife, and for our children.

Much like Jesus with the woman caught in adultery, Lindsey stepped into the circle with me. She recognized my shame and fear. She knew my painful secrets. In the face of shame, my wife became the voice of grace. She dared anyone holding stones to first look in the mirror before they threw the first at me. When others pushed me out, she pulled me closer. Choosing the path of unconditional love wasn't easy for her, but she did it anyway. When others refused to listen, she whispered, "Come home." That is the picture of grace.

Perfect love casts out all fear. And grace destroys shame.

But God still hasn't healed me. It makes some people uncomfortable, but the truth is, God's perfect love wasn't enough. Jesus didn't snap His fingers and fix my mess. It took practical, real life steps for my life to change. For me, healing came from honesty, medication, therapy, and hard work.

Yes, God was involved every step of the way, but it didn't happen at any altar. And it didn't happen magically, or overnight. In fact, my healing is still happening today.

Whether your story includes childhood sexual abuse, recovery from addiction, working through the aftermath of infidelity, or something completely different, grace is available for each of us. But grace isn't just a snapping of fingers and a shout of *Hallelujah*. Grace has a million different faces.

Sometimes grace is just the strength to keep living another day.

And Grace isn't a word that is only allowed to be spoken from pulpits and read in devotionals. In its simplest form, grace is a second chance. And at it's most complex, grace is a second chance. In my case, grace looked like a second chance from my wife. I had given up on myself after my suicide attempt, but Lindsey's trust in God's goodness was unwavering. For my wife, the messy middle includes me.

Why? Because life happens in the messy middle.

Reflection:

If you're in the messy middle today, where are you

finding goodness and beauty? Name one thing you notice today that lifts your head.

I LOVE JESUS, BUT...

5

...BUT I CRAVE COMMUNITY

By: Robert Vore

There is a liar.

I know, kind of an awkward topic, but there is. There is a liar living in your head. Our heads are really good at latching onto whatever lie we feel the most. It grabs it and repeats the lie, yelling in our faces again and again and again. *You are worthless. You only hurt people. You're ugly. You're stupid. The world would be better off without you.*

We fight it. We push back with other thoughts and truths and realities. Sometimes, we win. Sometimes, the truth prevails. *I matter. I have infinite worth. I am a beautiful light. The world needs my story and my life.*

But sometimes, we lose. We lose and we sink into our heads and we believe those lies and see proof of them playing like a reel. We *feel them* in every inch of us.

The lies are part of why community matters. Why vulnerability matters. We hear those words so often maybe we've forgotten what they mean, really.

Community matters because you need to be surrounded by people who speak the truth when your feelings tell you otherwise. Find a group of people who love you really well, even (especially) in the mess. They can scream truth into the darkness until the lies give way to light and you come to believe truth, see truth, *feel truth*, again.

And vulnerability matters because people can't help you fight if they don't know what you're fighting. The best people in the world can't help if they don't know. Nobody can fight lies with truth if they don't know what lies they're fighting.

We aren't created to fight alone. We were created to work and live and cry and celebrate alongside each other. Let people fight your lies with truth, and you do the same for them. Receive love, give love. Carry each others' burdens.

Fight together. Because we all matter.

Reflection:

When you're feeling particularly lonely, you need a support group. Who has earned the right to be in your inner circle? Write down their names here.

I LOVE JESUS, BUT...

6

...BUT SOMETIMES I WANT TO DIE

By: Steve Austin

Every September 21, I wonder where my notes went. The secrets they held, the deathbed confessions, the pain I was finally releasing. It was all on paper. But they are gone, and I am here, unsuccessful in my attempt to die.

Those letters still haunt me.

How do 20 pages of yellow legal paper just vanish? Later, when I was able, I called the hotel, the hospital, the ambulance service, the psych ward and the police department. No one ever saw them. They're just gone.

I spent two days drafting the most important letters of my life to all of my most important people.

The first was to Lindsey, my wife. It was the hardest to write. But it was sweet, it really was. I recalled our times traveling together, dreaming about changing the world while we sat on a moonlit back porch, driving through the countryside on lonely Saturday afternoons.

And I apologized for abandoning her and our baby boy. I was as genuinely sorry for leaving them as I was hell-bent on being delivered from my torture.

How can you apologize for the wrong you're about to commit? How can you possibly make right what will never be right? Five years earlier, I stood at an altar before God and promised to cherish and respect her until death. This was not what either of us had in mind.

I also wrote letters to my best friends, Michael and Gigi, to both of my brothers and to the youth group I was serving at the time, knowing I would forever be remembered as the youth pastor who committed suicide. I was fully aware that every sermon I'd ever preached, every article I'd ever written and every word of advice I'd ever offered would now be seen as fraudulent and empty.

I was the guy who constantly told stories of messy grace and unconditional love, of finding the hope of Jesus during dark nights. I was a phony, not worthy to ever stand behind a pulpit and offer hope and peace to anyone ever again.

Sharing my story always carries with it a bit of necessary weight, but I refuse to remain silent any longer, as people fall victim to the lie that there is no hope or help.

I even wrote a letter to my father-in-law, who still hates and distrusts me to this day. But I didn't write one to my Dad. He's never seemed to understand mental illness. But our issues went deeper than that. For six years, there had been a deep rift between us. A serious and hurtful indiscretion during his own mid-life crisis, along with a lifelong pattern of disengagement with his family, left me wondering if he would even care if I was gone.

Neither he nor my mom visited me in the hospital. I was glad I saved my ink.

Writing a note to my infant son, who would likely never remember me, nearly choked me with grief before I even began. I wanted a boy so badly. I was ready for kids long before Lindsey. When the two lines showed up on her pregnancy test, I screamed like Alabama had just won the National Championship. I had no doubts that baby would be my boy. I wanted a son, a legacy, one to impart wisdom and humor to. I wanted him, and I wanted to be his dad.

I just didn't want me.

I stared at the blank page, uncertain. It was the day before his first birthday. If I killed myself, he would only know about me based on the editorial comments of others. Would someone think to tell him about my sense of humor? Would Lindsey share how I used to sing to him in her belly? How I wept when he was delivered? How when he screamed on the warming table while nurses cleaned him, I sang to him again, and he stopped crying and turned toward me? He knew my voice. Even at birth, he knew my voice. Would someone remember to tell him that?

Would he ever watch the video of his grandpa and me singing a duet on my first Father's Day? He was there, sleeping on my chest the entire time, as we sang about being a holy example for my little boy. Would he know? Or would he only know me as a the one who left him, the coward who couldn't handle life? In the end, I decided it was better to abandon him forever than force him to suffer through being raised by a father who had lost his mind. When I finally finished the note to my little boy, I sighed hard, closed my Bible, and turned my attention to what was next.

Preparing to die is surreal.

I'm not sure how to even describe it. Imagine a dreamlike nightmare. Something fantastically terrible. In some ways I felt like a marionette, watching my hands scribe the darkest letters imaginable. I knew the choices I was making. I comprehended the secret plans I was devising, the dastardly deed that would forever mark my life as a failure. Yet it felt like my hands worked independent of my mind.

I knew my death would hurt my family and friends.

They'd be shocked and even miserable for a while. But life does go on. They would be OK without me. They would have no choice.

If you have never lived through the hell of sleepless nights, been strangled by the cold hands of anxiety, you can't understand why someone would want to die. You can't possibly "get it" if you've never heard that scream-whisper of depression that rarely backs down, or felt the sting of worthlessness, no matter how hard you work.

The constrictive wash of shame over your soul at a red light for absolutely no reason, the weight of guilt that you just cannot escape, no matter what you do. If you've never felt any of these things, you can't comprehend planning your death.

The statistics are shocking. About 42,773 people die by suicide in America each year. This equates to approximately 117 suicides per day or one death by suicide every 13 minutes. For every death, 25 more people attempt.

43,000 is a really big number. I would certainly lose count trying to count that high. And while I'm not a mathematician, I do know that one is much smaller than 43,000. The number one isn't nearly as impressive. One compared to 43,000 isn't earth-shattering.

Until one is your father.
Your mother.
Your child.
Your best friend. Your aunt.

When someone you love dies by suicide, it feels like 43,000 pounds of pain on your chest.

In Alabama, where I live, suicide was the second leading cause of death due to injury for adults. Right here, among people I know and love. Suicide is also the second leading cause of death for person aged 10 to 24 in the United States. *Young people. Kids.* Not "crazy" people.

Suicide respects no one. It has snuffed out bright lights like Robin Williams and Ernest Hemingway.

Closer to home, suicide robs families of teenagers and grandparents, steals teachers and pastors from communities and takes mothers away from their infants. It is a gift to survive it. Yet, for someone who has just survived a suicide attempt, it often feels like failure to be alive.

494,169 people went to a hospital for injuries due to self-harm in 2014. Those are just the documented cases. Thousands struggle in silence every single day. It could be the lady at your hair salon, the hero who just returned from a tour of duty, your child's teacher, your grandmother or your pastor.

The suicide epidemic is squeezing the life out of our families, churches and communities. This is the reason I am open about my story, why I've written a book about these struggles (*From Pastor to a Psych Ward*), why I speak out and why I encourage others too.

Two-thirds of people with mental illnesses don't seek treatment, and untreated depression is the number one cause of suicide. Sharing my story always carries with it a bit of necessary weight, but I refuse to remain silent any longer, as people fall victim to the lie that there is no hope or help. I tell my story not just for those who have failed a suicide attempt. My story can give hope and practical resources to anyone fighting a battle with anxiety, depression, bipolar disorder, obsessive compulsive disorder (OCD), post-traumatic stress disorder (PTSD) or paranoid personality disorder (PPD).

Suicide respects no one. It has snuffed out bright lights like Robin Williams and Ernest Hemingway. But closer to home, suicide robs families of teenagers and grandparents, steals teachers and pastors from communities and takes mothers away from their infants. It is a gift to survive it, but for someone who has just survived a suicide attempt, it often feels like failure to be alive.

I'm a pastor and I once attempted suicide because my brain has an illness, no different from heart disease or cancer. I require medication to function as normally as possible, and I have to visit a specialist to keep track of my progress.

The stigma surrounding mental illness, especially in Christian communities, keeps people locked in prisons of shame, refusing to admit that they need help. Yes Christians can and do struggle with mental illness. People need to know they are not alone, and you can still be a Christian and have a mental illness.

Together we can stop the stigma of mental illness and start saving lives.

Reflection:

Do you have an emergency plan? When you feel yourself being pulled beneath the tide, what's your escape plan? This is the perfect time to know who to call and where to go when you're feeling desperate.

7

...BUT LONELINESS IS MY KRYPTONITE

By: Robert Vore

When discussing addictions, the acronym HALT is frequently used to describe states of being you should avoid.

Hungry, Angry, Lonely, Tired.

Studies show that these are states in which people are more susceptible to their addictions. While I've never struggled with addiction, I've found that parts of this acronym apply to my mental and emotional well-being as well.

The last two, in particular, are where I run into trouble. Being lonely or tired throws my depression into overdrive in an incredibly short amount of time.

I spend a portion of my energy most days fighting lies in my head with truth. "What you feel vs. what you know" is a concept I reference fairly often. It goes something like this:

Brain: Wow, no one's texted you in like an hour. You must have no friends.

Me: Hmm, that doesn't seem quite right.

Brain: Pretty sure it is. In fact, given how much you value relationships, your crippling lack of friends who care enough to communicate with you is a big deal. It's just logic: you want relationships, but have literally none. No one cares about you. You're worthless.

Me: No. Logically, I don't have literally no friends. I have some really great friends who love me deeply, and I know that. And I know (regardless of temporary & misleading feelings) that I am loved. God loves me, my wife loves me, my family loves me, my friends love me, and my dog sure *as hell* loves me.

Brain: Ok, fine. But have you have no plans this weekend?

When I'm tired, I have no more energy to fight these

battles. When I'm tired, I'm also unlikely to go anywhere or do anything (because I'm tired, duh), which makes it worse because then *I'm all alone and my dumb brain has more ammunition to point out how alone and worthless I am.*

This happens more than I'd like. I have a propensity to jam a lot of things in my schedule and overcommit myself, because I'd rather be moving and doing than sitting still, then I crash and the lies in my head take over.

And all of that leads to loneliness. And loneliness is my Kryptonite.

It's why I hate the nighttime. For as long as I can remember, I've been awful at falling asleep. I remember getting in trouble consistently as a child for still being awake, reading Archie Comics when my parents went to bed. It's not like I was trying to stay up. I just can't fall asleep because my brain won't stop going.

The problem with taking hours to fall asleep is it gives

you an unprecedented amount of time to just lay there. Alone. In the dark. Thinking.

This is when my brain is at its worst.

Even now, when I'm home alone I have this overbearing feeling that I should be somewhere, doing something. I never know quite what to do when I have hours alone at the end of a day. It makes me feel alone. It makes me feel worthless because no one's around or talking to me or wanting anything to do with me (because *it's the middle of the damn night.*) It pulls me into the grey muck of my own head. I have the hardest time climbing out again because no one's around to yell truth into my darkness.

That's why, after reading a study on veterans who were given dogs to take care of so they'd feel less alone, I got a dog in college. I named him Nox, Latin for "night." I also fell asleep watching *Futurama* every night for years before I got married, and sometimes I still fall asleep to podcasts.

I also pack my schedule full and try to avoid having

too much time to myself.

Because when I'm still, and alone, and without distractions, I get lonely. Then I get sad. I don't get sad in a normal, something-bummed-me-out way. I get   sad   in   an I-can't-breathe-and-my-body-feels-heavy-and-it's-all-I -can-do-to-not-sink-into-myself kind of way.

If you don't understand that last sentence at all, I'm deeply and desperately sorry.

I'm sorry that there are times when it feels like it won't stop raining no matter what, and there are times where you're so desperate you would do *anything* but have no idea what that anything could even be, and I'm sorry that you and I share this bond. The sadness feels like a living breathing thing, but it's really just a lie, a pack of lies that fills your head and seeps downwards to effect the whole body until every inch of you feels contaminated and terrible and worthless. Words cannot express how sorry I am, and I know you know that because I know you feel the same way back.

Hold on. Because as much as I hate the night, as much as the darkness weighs on me and maybe on you, as much as I rail against the quiet and the still and the loneliness, this fact remains:

The sun does rise.

In the morning, the world sings with alarm clocks and morning news. Cities burst to life and *I am still here.* Even when I haven't wanted to be, I have managed to survive. That is no small feat. If you feel like all you've managed today is to make it through the night, please know there is no small victory in that. There is large, loud, celebration-style victory.

You are alive and you are breathing and *you are a whole damn miracle* because you have a heart that still beats in your chest.

Please stay. Please hold on. When it feels dark and quiet and lonely and you're trying to figure out how to feel comfortable in your own skin but just *can't* seem to get there, please stay anyway.

The sun will rise, in so many ways. *Please be here for*

it.

And in the meantime, know the things that make you heavy and the things that make you light. Get sleep, eat good foods, read a book or spend a night watching your favorite movie. Talk to the people around you. Hug your dog even though he doesn't like it (guilty).

There is no shame in doing what you need to be healthy, no disgrace in needing to keep yourself above water. You avoid foods that make you ill, this is no different. Fight to stay healthy. Fight to stay whole. Fight to stay.

I'll keep fighting if you will.

Reflection:

What is one thing you can do to practice good self-care the next time you feel hungry, angry, lonely, or tired?

I LOVE JESUS, BUT...

RESOURCES

Online Resources:

Active Minds

American Foundation for Suicide Prevention

CXMH Podcast

Crisis Text Line (Text 'Start' to 741-741)

DrugRehab.com

Heads Up Guys

GraceIsMessy.com

MentalHealth.gov

Mental Health America

Mental Health Grace Alliance

StigmaFighters.com

The Mighty

National Alliance on Mental Illness

NAMI Helpline

National Suicide Prevention Lifeline (1.800.273.8255 / 1.800.273.TALK)

Robert-Vore.com

Book Recommendations:

- Troubled Minds: Mental Illness and the Church's Mission
- Myths About Suicide
- Why People Die By Suicide
- Counseling Suicidal People: A Therapy of Hope
- Night Falls Fast: Understanding Suicide
- From Pastor to a Psych Ward: Recovery from a Suicide Attempt is Possible
- Madness: American Protestant Responses to Mental Illness
- Self Care for the Wounded Soul: 21 Days of Messy Grace
- Some Things You Keep

Basic Self Care Checklist

☐ Breakfast & meds.

☐ Feed your soul & move your body.

☐ How's your self talk?

☐ Practice boundaries.

☐ Get good rest.

cxmhpodcast.com

I LOVE JESUS, BUT...

I LOVE JESUS, BUT...

I LOVE JESUS, BUT...

I LOVE JESUS, BUT...

34406758R00039

Made in the USA
Lexington, KY
22 March 2019